Spirituality Made Simple

Owen Waters

Table of Contents

Introduction

You are a spiritual being, living in a material world and secretly endowed with infinite intelligence and creative power.

You only have to look within, to your true being, to connect with spiritual levels of consciousness. The more familiar you become with these expanded levels of consciousness, the more potential becomes available to you for the creation of a better life and a better world.

There are two phases in the development of human consciousness, both at the individual level and in society as a whole. First, the material stages are experienced, then the spiritual stages.

Humanity has devoted much of the past century to the stage of development that focuses on the intellect. Today, however, people are migrating in droves to the next stage of human growth, which is heart-centered consciousness. Once people become accustomed to thinking with their hearts as well as their heads, they stand at the gateway of spiritual consciousness.

Spirituality is the development of higher consciousness. Spiritual consciousness begins with heart-centered awareness and the increasing sense that there is a universal Spirit of God or an all-pervasive intelligence behind all things.

We all have an inner connection to the universe and to the ultimate intelligence which created the universe. With the emergence of the first spiritual stage of consciousness, we become aware of that connection. We begin to sense that it is something sacred and, yet, it is also a part of us. It is a universal yearning for unity with that from which we originally came. It is a call to begin the journey back to our ultimate spiritual home.

Spirituality brings deeper meaning and fulfillment into people's lives by opening up the higher faculties that lay dormant during the material stages of consciousness. These higher faculties include insight, empathy, and creativity:

Insight

With rapidly-expanding intuitive insight, you gain a greater sense of knowing about the true nature of any situation.

Empathy

You find yourself developing a sense of connection with all of Creation. This happens because you are connected within to spiritual realms that are filled with love, light, and joy.

Creativity

Higher creativity is the ability to reshape your reality around a new intention. Spiritual consciousness is the key to the real power in creating a new reality. With it, you can create a better life and make the world a better place.

Three Easy Steps to Spirituality

Three Easy Steps
to Spirituality

With the three steps revealed in this book, spirituality, or the development of higher consciousness, becomes literally as easy as *1-2-3*. Being based upon the Universal Law of Creation, these three steps are inherently powerful and effective.

These steps will help you through the gateway to spiritual consciousness and then into contact with the higher states of inspiration, wisdom and creativity that exist within your true, inner being.

These are the days of historic, spiritual transformation. People are aware that the world is changing faster than ever. This is no basic awakening or simple renaissance. Today's *Shift* is the big one. It is transforming humanity from the realms of basic, material awareness into the realms of spiritual awareness.

Every day that passes, more and more people are awakening to the heart-centered consciousness that is the hallmark of the New Reality.

The first step of spiritual consciousness is the focusing of your mind upon your spiritual nature. This becomes much easier to achieve with a full understanding of basic spiritual principles.

Step 1

Look Up

Step 1 - Look Up

Recognize your spiritual nature. Know that you are a spiritual being living in a physical world. The real, immortal you is your inner being or soul consciousness. Several times each day, take a few moments to connect with, and remember, your true nature as a spiritual being.

Remind yourself that the universe was created by the all-present, all-aware consciousness which is behind all things. This infinite presence or beingness, this *Infinite Being*, created the universe in order to experience itself from all possible perspectives.

You are this consciousness. You are an expression of Infinite Being, experiencing life from one individual point of view. Just as each snowflake is unique, so is each person. We are the eyes, ears, and hearts of Infinite Being as it experiences life from all possible viewpoints.

The objective of living on earth as a human is to gain experience while finding our way back to the ultimate state of consciousness from which we originally came.

The Ultimate State of Higher Consciousness

The Ultimate State of Higher Consciousness

Infinite Being is the ultimate state of higher consciousness.

The entire universe sprang from the original, infinite awareness called Infinite Being, the Absolute, or The All That Is.

Infinite Being is a state of consciousness, not a being. We are all a part of it. It consists of all of us and everything else that exists in all states of consciousness throughout the entire universe.

Life is like a train ride. We pass through it, gaining experience and, hopefully, enjoying the ride. One day we will reach our destination – oneness with the state of Infinite Being from which we originally came. In the meantime, the purpose of life is to enjoy the ride and to learn from all the experiences that it has to offer along the way.

The better we understand the journey called life, the sooner we master all that it has to offer and the sooner we can move along into the next phase of our constant evolution back to our spiritual source.

Answers to Timeless Mysteries

Answers to
Timeless Mysteries

One of the great benefits of today's emerging new consciousness is that the old mysteries of life are dissolving before our eyes; mysteries like:

Who are we?

Why are we here?

What is the meaning of life?

These answers to these ancient mysteries are becoming more and more clear with today's emerging new consciousness.

They are best answered by first going back to the original Creation to see how Infinite Being managed to create the physical universe from empty nothingness.

The Secret of Creation

The Secret of Creation

By utilizing the Universal Law of Creation, you can create new realities that improve your life and enhance your ability to help others. This is the law that was used to create the entire universe, so it should come as no surprise that, correctly used, it is both powerful and effective.

While Infinite Being is the ever-present ground state of passive awareness which exists throughout Creation, the Creator is the action-oriented aspect of Infinite Being. The Creator aspect was brought into being for the task of creating the universe so that Infinite Being could experience itself from all possible perspectives.

The only tool at the disposal of the Creator in making the universe was consciousness. Therefore, everything in the universe consists of consciousness – people, rocks, plants and planets – and, because they consist of consciousness, they all have some degree of awareness.

Creation was made possible when the Creator divided its consciousness into two complementary aspects – thought and feeling. It then intertwined these aspects and set them into motion in ways that created everything that was needed to develop life as we know it today.

The universe, you, and everything around you consists of 100% consciousness.

Life is but a dream, and each one of us is here to change the dream in our own unique way.

Recreate your dream to realize all of your potential using the Universal Law of Creation.

The Universal Law of Creation

Creation = Thought + Feeling + Motion

The three *Spirituality Made Simple* steps to spiritual living are structured using the Universal Law of Creation.

Look Up – focus your thoughts on your spiritual nature

Look In – find spiritual consciousness through the gateway of the heart

Look Out – take action to express your inner joy and your unique purpose in life

The Meaning
of Life

The Meaning of Life

You are an expression of Infinite Being as it experiences itself from all possible perspectives. Your perspective is unique, as is everyone else's. That is the point of the whole exercise – for Infinite Being to experience life from as many perspectives as possible.

In order to best support this primary mission of human experience, we need to both celebrate our own uniqueness and support others in their efforts to develop their own skills and talents. Unity is our spiritual nature, yet it is found through celebrating our diversity in the common cause of developing our potential to the fullest.

The One is the All and, as parts of the All, we are essentially the One. At the deepest level of consciousness, we are Infinite Being.

Everyone's path is unique because that's the way life was designed. There is no one-size-fits-all philosophy. However, we can learn about the universal laws that will help us achieve our potential in life.

Your mind is non-physical and therefore has higher capabilities than your physical brain. Your mind is immortal and it grows with experience.

We are each on our own pathways back to the One source from which we originally came. To get there, we continually grow in consciousness by experiencing life.

The meaning of life is to grow in consciousness.

Your True
Inner Nature

Your True Inner Nature

Today, we are just beginning to appreciate the enormous scale of Creation. In the Middle Ages, most people worked the land. They rarely ventured far away from their place of birth, so their concept of the world was quite small. Likewise, their concept of God the Creator was small in scale. To them, God was an all-powerful, wise, elderly, human-like figure who lived somewhere above them.

People, at the time, didn't realize the massive size of the planet upon which they stood. To them, most of their universe could be seen from the top of the nearest hill. Today, with cosmology and the Hubble telescope to help us, our view of the size of the universe has been stretched farther and farther.

What we have learned, since the Middle Ages, includes these realizations:

1. The Earth is not the center of the universe. Apparently, when this was discovered, it came as quite a shock.

2. The Earth is round. This was excellent news at the time: No more worrying that you might take to sea and sail off the edge of the world!

3. The Earth travels around the Sun. This means that, while modern-day life on Earth may seem to be expensive at times, it does come with the added bonus, once a year, of a free trip around the Sun!

4. The Sun is over a million times bigger than the Earth.

5. There are 200 billion other suns in our own galaxy.

6. There are well over 100 billion galaxies in the universe.

7. As big as the universe is, in order for God to be everywhere, God has to be bigger still.

When you view God as Infinite Being, the All That Is, or the Absolute, you have a sense of scale that still encompasses all of Creation, no matter how far the universe stretches. The infinity of Infinite Being encompasses all of space. The Creator aspect of Infinite Being created all of space within its consciousness.

The question is, where does the individual fit into this enormous scale of Creation?

The deeper into your own consciousness you travel, the more you become aware that the All is One. That the infinite possibilities are all expressions of the One. Beneath all expression is just the One, and the One is Infinite Being.

In the 'All is One' ultimate reality, you are a viewpoint of the One. Nothing can be truly separate from the One.

It can only be another facet of the One.

Regardless of how huge the universe is, you are fully connected to the Creator of the stars, the planets, and all of life. We are examples of the infinite variety which is Creation and each one of us is an essential part of the whole.

If it were somehow possible for you to disappear from the universe – and it isn't – then Creation would be infinity minus one, and that is no longer infinity. You have always existed and, in whatever form that suits you at the time, you always will.

Because people are an expression of Infinite Being, the potential within each and every one of us is infinite. There are no limits to what you will become in your journey back to your original spiritual home. And, there need be no limits in the life that you are now living.

A society that encourages all of its members to develop their full potential will be more supportive, creative and productive. Everyone will benefit.

Just think of your true human potential this way;

Infinite Being, infinite potential.

Destiny and
Free Will

Destiny and Free Will

In the Old Reality, things were seen as opposites – hot or cold, black or white, good or bad, this way or that way. In the expanded view of New Reality consciousness, life is seen in a unified way. Opposite sides of the coin are viewed, not as polar opposites, but rather as just being different aspects of the one coin.

In the New Reality view of the world, the opposite extremes of hot and cold become variable degrees of warmth. Black and white become, instead, endless shades of gray. Good and bad become different shades of human nature and these can be viewed without the judgment and fear that comes with Old Reality, polarized thinking.

In the Old Reality, destiny and free will were seen as mutually exclusive. The reasoning was that, if destiny exists, then it controls everything and, therefore, free will does not exist. On the other hand, you can prove that free will does exist by making a choice. So, as the thinking goes, if free will does exist, then there can be no destiny.

But, wait. Perhaps that choice of "free will" was really a pre-destined one. Perhaps the person was destined to make that choice all along, so the experience of choice was just an illusion. At this point, people usually give up on the whole question because it has turned into one of those brain teasers, like asking which came first – the chicken or the egg.

Brain teasers keep your mind in an endless loop until you step back from the situation and see it in a wider perspective. The new, wider perspective allows for the inclusion of non-materialistic factors. In deciding whether the chicken or the egg came first, for example, you just have to step back and see that the Creator designed the chicken to be self-perpetuating.

When you step back and see destiny and free will from a wider perspective, you realize that nothing has to be absolute. If every event in your life were pre-ordained, there would be no such thing as free will or self-determination. As we do have free will, destiny cannot be fixed.

Destiny is therefore variable, not fixed. Destiny and free will both exist as interwoven facets of your life. Like threads in a tapestry, they interact with each other and blend to form the outcomes that are the events in your life.

Your destiny is created by plans that you made at a soul level of consciousness. Before you were born, you made your main plan for this life. Then, the minute you were born, the rules of the game demanded that you also get a case of amnesia about the whole arrangement. Such is the game of life in the physical realm.

However, at night when you go to sleep, you have the chance to visit the deepest levels of human consciousness and review how the original plan is unfolding and make changes to your plan if desired. When you return to your physical body and awake in the morning, amnesia strikes again. Within seconds of your conscious mind returning into your physical brain, you forget both the surface dreams and the deep experiences of the night.

Amnesia may be a part of the game we are playing in this life, but inner guidance is always available to anyone who pays attention to it. Your intuition is your link to your soul, or inner being, which is also linked to the rest of the universe and all levels of Creation.

You are never left alone to fumble in the darkness of a purely physical life. Your inner being is always there with you, expressing itself through the quiet whisperings of intuitive information. Thanks to this inner compass of knowing, you can always sense which choice feels right. You can always tell when your life is running on plan, and you can tell equally well if you've become temporarily distracted from your plan. You always have the means to be right on course, or get back on course, and explore the fascinating themes that make up your life plan.

The most productive use of free will is to explore your true potential within the themes of your life, thus gaining the greatest possible experience from your life plan.

Destiny is an influence that comes from your inner plan. There is nothing absolute about your destiny.

It's a pressure which constantly seeks the best route to unfold into manifestation.

Free will provides the means to manifest that destiny in a way that provides the learning that you came here to acquire in this life.

Destiny is variable. It adapts to new circumstances in your life every day. As destiny unfolds, you feel it within as a sense of being a part of the flow of life, of manifesting your potential in the way that you planned for this day and that you planned for this life.

Destiny is the plan. Free will is the action. Experience is the result.

That's what being human is.

Step 2

Look In

Step 2 - Look In

The gateway to spiritual consciousness is through the heart.

The Creator designed the human experience to consist of twelve stages of evolving consciousness. These range all the way from basic survival to the ultimate state of spiritual consciousness and they are defined later in the chapter, *The Twelve Stages of Human Consciousness.*

Much of the 20th century was devoted to the fifth stage of human consciousness, which is intellectual development. Today, people are migrating in droves to the next stage of human growth, which is heart-centered consciousness.

When a person focuses their intellect through the lens of heart-centered consciousness, they see how much the world needs help and healing rather than the old ways of competition and destruction. The initial stage of heart-centered consciousness produces a constructive, global outlook. It also places a person just one short step from the later stage of heart-centered consciousness and the dawning of spiritual awareness.

"Love your neighbor as yourself" is a guideline that has been with us since the early days of human development. Today, it's no longer a distant ideal to be sought. The mass shift to heart-centered consciousness means that unconditional love now comes to people naturally.

The complete love and acceptance of yourself and others is the heartbeat of the New Reality.

Feeling unconditional love towards others is the key to successful, meaningful interactions with everyone with whom you meet in any situation. Feeling unconditional love towards yourself fosters a healthy sense of self-esteem which builds a positive reality based upon mutual support.

Even if there are outer behaviors that need improvement in yourself or others, it is unconditional love that is the key that will find the solutions that will bring positive transformation to those behaviors.

Once you begin to think with an open heart, you are stepping from basic human consciousness into the spiritual stages of human development. This is exactly what we came to earth to accomplish because finding spirituality is fundamental to the human experience. It may take courage to move into heart-centered consciousness, but once you acquire the expanded view of a life filled with love, you will never want to step back to the way things were.

You will soon find that any worries or fears that arise in your life can be transformed by the greatest power in the universe – that of unconditional love. It is the power of love that holds the universe together. It is a force of attraction that permeates every cell of your body and constantly reminds you of the love of the Creator for all of life.

The Evolution
of
Consciousness

The Evolution of Consciousness

The human race was designed to evolve through 12 progressive stages of consciousness, all the way from caveman to cosmic consciousness.

In my first book, *The Shift: The Revolution in Human Consciousness*, I showed the exact correspondence between the historical stages of the development of human society and the different energy centers in the human body.

The symmetry of this aspect of Creation showed even more when I found that the 12 stages of consciousness also resonate exactly to the 12 notes of the musical C-octave. This was a clear indication that the 12 stages of the evolution of consciousness were designed into the human experience.

Knowing that our journey through human experience was designed, and therefore generally pre-destined, we can gain much from studying the map of that 12-stage journey. With a map, you can see, not only where you have been, but where you are going next.

The Twelve
Stages of
Human
Consciousness

The Twelve Stages of Human Consciousness

The 12-Stage Map of Human Consciousness consists of two tiers of six stages each. It begins with a material tier of six stages and then progresses into a spiritual tier of another six stages. The 12 stages are:

The Material Tier

1. Survival: Maintaining physical existence

2. Tribal: Gathering into groups for protection

3. Courage: Adventure and exploration

4. Conformity: Creating order out of chaos through hierarchical control

5. Intellect: Basic mental development; physical science

6. Community: The initial stage of heart-centered consciousness; putting the greater good above the self

The Spiritual Tier

7. Love: The later stage of heart-centered consciousness; the first step in spiritual consciousness; awareness that you are a spiritual being

8. Inspiration: Intuitive reason; attunement with the age-old wisdom and unconditional joy of your soul

9. Creativity: Development of a greater ability to create powerful new realities; higher mental development

10. Enlightenment: The goal of spiritual seekers; direct access to the secrets of the universe

11. Angelic: The realm of angels and avatars

12. Cosmic: Cosmic consciousness; the peak state of human experience

The Twelve
Human
Energy Centers

The Twelve Human Energy Centers

Tradition has it that there are just seven major energy centers, or chakras ("*shack-ras*"), in the human energy system. Each chakra is an energetic vortex tuned to handle a specific frequency band of consciousness and life energy.

It is less commonly known that five of these chakras have two sides; they have forward faces and backward faces. The inclusion of the total of all twelve chakra faces is key to this study because they correspond exactly to the twelve stages of human consciousness.

Society advances through these stages, exploring each one in turn, as do individuals. Our modern era is historically unique as we are transitioning from the material tier of consciousness to the spiritual tier.

The pioneering element within society today is becoming inspired to explore the new frontier of spiritual consciousness and become the trailblazers of higher human potential.

Stage	Type	Chakra Face
1	Survival	Root chakra
2	Tribal	Sex chakra – front face
3	Courage	Sex chakra – back face
4	Conformity	Solar plexus chakra – front face
5	Intellect	Solar plexus chakra – back face
6	Community	Heart chakra – front face
7	Love	Heart chakra – back face
8	Inspiration	Throat chakra – front face
9	Creativity	Throat chakra – back face
10	Enlightenment	Third eye chakra – front face
11	Angelic	Third eye chakra – back face
12	Cosmic	Crown chakra

The Twelve Chakra Faces
as Energy Vortexes

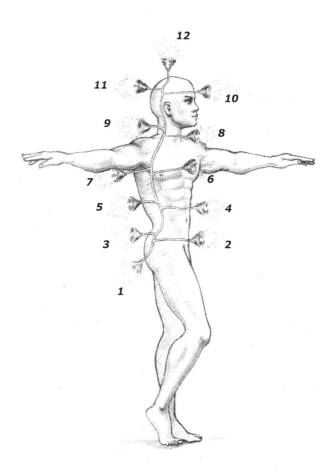

The Future of Human Evolution

The Future of Human Evolution

Notice how stages 6 and 7 are both heart-centered stages and, yet, stage 6 is in the material tier while stage 7 is in the spiritual tier. This is why the gateway to spiritual consciousness is through the heart.

Once a person reaches stage 7, the entire potential of the spiritual tier lies before them and their personal growth can increase by leaps and bounds.

Having a map of the twelve stages of consciousness means that we can now predict the nature of the future of human evolution. Each person, or group of people, has the choice of experiencing the current popular stage or they can move ahead of the mainstream, becoming modern-day pioneers in exploring the next stages of human growth.

Access to stages 8 and 9 will open up a huge wave of constructive creativity. These stages contain the vision and the ability for people to remake the world as a place of deep and lasting beauty. Constraints that we take for granted today will begin to dissolve. For example, when we unravel the secrets of instantaneous travel through space, we will gain enormous freedom of movement.

Stages 10 and 11 are the stages of enlightened wisdom. Even glimpses of these rarefied levels of consciousness during deep meditation allow much wisdom to flow into the awareness. The achievement of stage 12 is the ultimate, long sought-after state of cosmic consciousness, which is the true pinnacle of human potential.

The Nature of
Unconditional
Love

The Nature of Unconditional Love

The purpose of being human, as we shift into the New Reality, includes learning about heart-centered consciousness.

The universe is, by its very design, filled with the love of the Original Creator. Universal love is the aspect of Original Consciousness which holds Creation together. In the Original Creation, Infinite Being divided its consciousness into two complementary aspects – thought and feeling – and then set them into motion.

The love of the Original Creator forms the very fabric of space. No material thing and no part of "empty" space is devoid of that love. Universal love is literally everywhere. However, the human condition is only consciously affected by this love when it is channeled into the human realm through its use by humans.

We are here on Earth to learn how to translate universal love into human form.

Once universal love has been transformed through the consciousness of any individual human being, it affects the global mind atmosphere of Earth. We all share constant access to this global mind. While we initiate thoughts and feelings on our own, we also receive thoughts and feelings from the global mind. We sometimes alter these by our own thought, sometimes not, and then pass them back into the global mind. Even though we are typically not accustomed to conscious telepathy, our subconscious and superconscious minds are fully telepathic. We constantly receive and transmit thoughts and feelings subconsciously from and to the global mind atmosphere.

When a person experiences heart-centered consciousness, they radiate a type of consciousness which is very different to basic emotion. Heart-centered consciousness is a state of unconditional love. It is not a product of emotional like or dislike. Once started, nothing in physical reality affects the flow of unconditional love. It is something that just is, regardless of the circumstances.

Unconditional love is something that flows through your heart when you reach up above day-to-day consciousness, tune into your heart-awareness and allow the universal love energy to flow through you. Heart-centered consciousness always sees the elegant solution to the sorrows that can arise from basic human emotions.

Unconditional love allows, accepts and supports. It is not something you try to do. It just flows when you allow it to enter your heart and take your consciousness above the cares of daily reality and into an expanded vista of awareness.

Each time you radiate unconditional love into the global mind atmosphere, you upgrade the entire human experience, taking humanity yet one more step into the unfolding New Reality.

The Gateway
to Spiritual
Consciousness

The Gateway to Spiritual Consciousness

Love is the saving grace of all of humanity. We contact this primal energy in our finest moments. From the moment a baby is born, it is enshrouded in the unselfish love of its mother. From the moment a person springs into action to save others from peril, their own thoughts of survival are 'overlighted' by the love and caring that shines from their heart.

When a person looks back on their life, they see that one thing that mattered the most: Love. Pure, unadulterated, unconditional love.

It is the source of compassion. It is the energy of caring for others. It is the binding force which holds together the entire universe, and it flows through you whenever you simply allow it.

Love is the gateway to spiritual consciousness. It is through activation of the spiritual heart that we pass into a whole new world of expansion and joy. In the realms of spiritual consciousness, we find peace, bliss, and continual inspiration. In the realms of spiritual consciousness, we expand our view of life to see the issues that are important to the soul. We can then see how love can heal and how we can and should spend the time to spread a little more love in the world every day, even if it is simply done in silent prayer for the well-being of others.

Let your heart open to love each and every day. When you are attuned to the natural flow of love throughout the universe, you then feel the natural flow of energy within your own being. Your senses of insight and timing develop to help you achieve more and to succeed easily at the tasks that are important to you.

The flow of love is critical to life. Without the all-pervasive love of the Creator which fills the universe, nothing would exist. For centuries, humankind has been playing a game where love and inner inspiration have been blocked off and ignored. Today, the tide is turning and people are opening up to this wonderful flow of natural energy.

Remember the love within, especially when outer circumstances seem dark. Remember that love is the gateway to the higher realms of consciousness where answers can be found to meet every challenge that life presents.

Tune into love. It will never let you down. Instead, it will set your spirit free to explore the realms of consciousness which offer greater vistas of awareness, greater peace of mind, and a sense of constant joy.

Reconnecting with Love

Reconnecting with Love

With the ups and downs of life, there can be times when your connection to a universe of love seems distant. The opposite of love is fear and it appears in many forms. Depression, anxiety, guilt and anger are all expressions of fear and they can flourish in the absence of love.

Fortunately, fear has a simple antidote. Love dissolves fear, so you need to know how to bring its feeling back when it has temporarily gone away.

Gratitude is one type of expression of love which has enormous power. Gratitude is invoked when you mentally send love to those whom you appreciate. It becomes especially powerful when you send your gratitude to your concept of God the Creator for all the good things in your life and for life itself, because God will reciprocate with uplifting energies. That one step you take towards God really does bring a reaction of two steps towards you.

Gratitude takes you right out of your personal sphere of consciousness and into an expanded view of the universe.

In this way, it raises you far above the petty fears that still try to haunt people in the everyday world. Gratitude is one of the most beautiful secrets in spiritual life. It is an expression of love, and love flows through all forms of manifestation. Without love, life in the universe cannot exist. Love is the universal force of preservation which holds Creation in manifestation.

When you allow your heart to open to the universe's flow of love, gratitude comes with that flow. Gratitude for being alive, for just existing, for just being in the flow of the adventure of life. Gratitude for the Sun that gives us life. Gratitude for the Creation of the Earth as our home in this great cosmos. Gratitude for the people that you love, and for those who share your journey through life.

Gratitude flows unimpeded from an open heart. When you allow it, gratitude will flow as freely as the sunshine, unobstructed by judgments or conditions.

Use the following affirmation and see what happens. Keep repeating it and, each time, think more about what the words mean.

The Gratitude Affirmation adds new meaning to the term, *quality of life*. It really works! Try it now.

Gratitude Affirmation

I am grateful for life
And all that I love
I am grateful for the Earth
And the Sun up above
I am grateful for my spirit
And my inner being
For the One that I express
And the joy of this feeling

When you awaken each day, even before you get out of bed, think of ten things for which you are grateful. Finish your reflections with the Gratitude Affirmation and, each day, you'll feel inspired to have the best day ever!

Step 3

Look Out

Step 3 - Look Out

Outward action is the third key to spiritual living. In this section, we will examine the different facets of action that create spiritual growth in the New Reality.

With heart-centered consciousness comes self-respect, the desire to help others, and the confidence to develop your greatest talents and put those to work. By doing work that you love, you transform your life into one filled with inner joy and you also improve the lives of the people you serve through your work.

When you see life through the lens of your heart, you see how your innermost joy and passion continually prompt you to develop your own unique talents. When you recognize those talents, you can acquire the skills that bring them into active expression. When you become able to spend your working days doing what you love and loving what you do, then your life becomes a constant experience of heartfelt joy.

The inspiring guideline stated by Jesus, "Do unto others as you would have them do unto you," is one that becomes second nature in today's emerging New Reality.

A heart-centered person simply wouldn't do anything to hurt another. Nor would they want anyone to receive less than fair value for their goods and services.

You can bring light and joy into the world by engaging in heartfelt action and doing work that you love.

You can also make a positive difference by using spiritual energy to heal the world and make it a better place.

Living in the
New Reality

Living in the New Reality

Just as there were rules to succeeding in the Old Reality, there are rules which are best adopted when taking action in the New Reality.

The Old Reality was about gaining courage and developing intellect. The New Reality is about unconditional love and inner wholeness.

Wholeness is personally-inspired integrity without the "shoulds" that others may try to impose upon you.

The frequency of consciousness in the New Reality is heart-centered. Unconditional love comes naturally; you need only let it flow through your heart and allow that energy to be who you are.

When you shift to the expanded consciousness of the New Reality, the universe reorganizes itself around you to reflect that higher reality. Externally-imposed rules are replaced by internal, love-based choices.

To become whole is to become harmoniously fully-functional. In such a reality, you treat yourself and others with unconditional love and care. To care less than that for yourself, or less than that for others, would mean being less than whole.

Intuitive
Reason

Intuitive Reason

Intuition brings you direct information on the true nature of any situation.

Once you make a habit of looking within and focusing on your spiritual nature, you open up your awareness to the intuitive information that can come from your soul consciousness. Intuitive insight is available to both men and women and, with its development, you can achieve more than you have ever imagined possible.

The conscious, reasoning mind assesses a situation using the physical senses as well as past information. Intuitive reason is possible when you include intuitive information in the process. Intuition comes from your inner, soul consciousness and is directly tuned into the thoughts and energies that surround any situation.

Intuition adds to your knowledge and understanding of a situation, allowing your actions to achieve objectives with greater ease and harmony.

With intuition, you know *what* action will best work and *when*.

Intuition is your doorway to direct information on the consciousness of people, places, and events. It can also warn you about danger ahead and reveal what hidden risks you could avoid in order to stay safe.

Intuition prompts you to take actions which will help you in ways that you had not been able to detect using the physical senses alone. It also puts you in touch with the natural flow of unfolding situations so that you can adapt to them and, therefore, succeed with relatively effortless action.

Effortless
Action

Effortless Action

There is a flow to events; a timing that, when under-stood, makes tasks much easier to achieve. The key to gaining this information is to tune into your inner, soul consciousness.

This inner work need not be a one-way street of receiv-ing inside information. You can also take the initiative by using the principle of effortless action. Instead of trying to make something happen by the usual efforts of planning, willpower and determination, you begin by going within and seeing the action as accomplished.

When you begin by seeing the action as completed, and creating a feeling of completion, something very differ-ent happens. The action doesn't mysteriously become accomplished by magic or by non-effort, but you experi-ence a state of flow which enables you to move through the task with ease, grace and incredible efficiency.

The easiest way to invoke a state of flow is to go within, attune with your inner being and the intended task. Then, come out into the world of action and follow your intuitive guidance every step of the way until the task becomes physically completed.

This is how synchronicity happens and you notice coin-cidences becoming commonplace in your life. People, ideas and resources all come together at the exact right time and in the right place because flow is an orchestra-tion of the many, not just the one.

Like water finding the shortest and easiest path down a slope, your intuition will reveal the shortest and easiest route to the successful completion of any task.

The Mirror
of Life

The Mirror of Life

Karma, in the popular view, is often perceived as the bogeyman of Eastern philosophy, as the stick that punishes you for doing the wrong thing. In reality it is much simpler than that, and it carries no judgmental overtone at all. Jesus eloquently stated this universal law to the people of his time by saying, "As you sow, so shall you reap."

Karma is simply reflectance. Reflectance is a property of the universe. Therefore, life is a mirror which reflects what you project. This principle of reflectance or karma states that life reflects your beliefs, emotions and actions. The stronger these are, the more apparent it becomes that life is a mirror of whatever you project.

Whenever you change the way you view life, the universe, just like a mirror, reflects your new view of reality. This may not occur instantaneously as, often, circumstances do not allow the new reflection to immediately manifest. In this case, the new reality is held, like a pressure within the aura of your body's subtle magnetic field. You then walk around in life, surrounded by this magnetic potential, your *karmic pattern*, as it influences your circumstances to adapt into a form where the new reality will be able to manifest and operate.

Reflectance, sooner or later, produces manifestation. Therefore, if you don't like something in your life, the most powerful way to change it is to discover how, consciously or subconsciously, you have generated that reflection. Then change your point of view – the beliefs, viewpoints and energies that you put into your life – so that the reflection is changed.

It's just like the law in physics: "For every action, there is an opposite and equal reaction." This law goes much deeper than just a law of mechanical motion. It is how the universe is designed at all levels.

When a person moves from material consciousness into heart-centered consciousness, it may appear that their old karmic pattern has ended. It has. In its place is a reflection of the new person and their unconditional love for all. The reflection is different, but, as a fundamental law, karma never ceases to exist. The property of reflectance is interwoven into the fabric of the living universe.

Without a law of balance, the universe would not stay in balance. Karma is a design feature of the universe and it will continue for as long as the universe exists.

Reflectance is an entirely automatic process. There is no judge. No one looms over you, threatening retribution for imaginary sins. However, because this law of life is automatic, you have to be the one to initiate change. It will not come to you until you take the initiative, until you create the action so that there can be a reaction.

If you seek more happiness from life, the mirror of life will reflect more happiness back upon you, just as soon as you decide, within yourself, to become a happier person. Then, it will reflect your new reality.

Your power lies in how you respond to the circumstances which have been created in your life. Circumstances, within themselves, are inherently neutral. It is human judgment that assigns positive and negative values to those circumstances. One of the paradoxes of life is that the challenge of difficult times can produce the most happiness and wisdom in the end.

Remember that if "bad" circumstances are affecting you, it is often not because of some "bad" way that you thought or behaved in the past, but it may be because you planned your life so that it would present certain challenges. How you respond to these challenges is the whole point of the exercise. The strongest steel is that which is quenched from great heat and the most compassionate heart is one which has seen great suffering in the world.

Your viewpoint is your response to the picture that life presents, and it is totally under your control. Your viewpoint determines what energies you will put into life and, therefore, what the mirror of life will reflect back to you.

Life is a mirror. Smile, and it will immediately smile back at you!

The Fast Track
to Spiritual
Development

The Fast Track
to Spiritual Development

Once you acquire heart-centered consciousness, the secret to rapid spiritual development becomes apparent.

Paradoxically, the secret to rapid growth is this: It isn't what you do to develop yourself that counts so much as what you do to help others. Spiritual service to others brings an immediate reflection from the mirror of life and you advance automatically in a balanced and graceful manner.

Contrast that to the mental attitude of the Old Reality, with its self-serving orientation: To use the small business marketplace as an example, there are those who focus primarily on ways that they might extract more money from the marketplace and there are those who focus primarily on the needs of their customers.

The people who succeed most easily are the ones who say, "I can see how to provide those goods, or services, better and cheaper than they are right now." Their attitude is one that focuses more towards the concept of service to others. The reaction to their giving more value is one of automatic prosperity. The difference comes from an attitude of service to others versus service to self.

The same principle applies to both physical and spiritual service. Physical prosperity comes as the reaction from physically serving others better. Spiritual development comes as the reaction from helping others in spiritual ways. Fortunately, with the knowledge we now have available to us, spiritual service to the world has never been easier.

The world cries out to be helped and healed in countless ways. Ignorance, needless suffering and strife are all symptoms of the remaining Old Reality consciousness in the world.

As you are about to see, you personally have the power to change such conditions. In nearly five decades of spiritual research, the most effective and balanced practice for spiritual growth that I have ever found is one I learned in my early days in 1972.

The Transformative Power of Healing Energy

The Transformative Power of Healing Energy

In order to appreciate the potential of this practice, take your mind up into the vastness of the cosmos and imagine a universe filled with life-giving energy.

Imagine all the power that the Creator funnels into the universe in order to meet its energy needs. Energy is constantly needed on many levels, including physical energy, universal life force, and mind energy. Galaxies, suns and planets need to keep turning. People need warmth, light and mental energy in order to function and experience life.

All consciousness in existence is powered by a constant cascade of life-giving energy that comes from the great Central Sun of Creation. From there, it is distributed through the cosmic network of billions of galaxies and their suns. The Sun is a portal for the energy that originates from the Creator and supports all life in the universe.

The highest form of energy that we can contact – the love and power of God – is not some imaginary form of wishful thinking. It is an ever-present energy which is supplied to you and through you.

Spiritual energy is a power that you can attract, condition, and use to heal the world.

There is no lack of the love and power of God on this planet. There is only the lack of people knowing how to use this energy for the spiritual advancement of themselves and the world.

If you lift up your mind to the Creator, and to the love and life energy which surrounds you now, you can feel that divine power filling your consciousness and every part of your being. Breathe it into your body like an energetic white mist that builds into a vibrant white light within you and charges every cell of your being with its life-giving energy.

Next, dedicate that energy to world healing and direct it to flow out into the world from the heart chakra area in front of your chest. Life energy responds to any mental pressure that you apply to it. Send it out as a beam of heart-centered, sacred energy and it will instantly inspire others. They, too, will affect the global mind atmosphere, changing the balance of humanity's thought in a positive direction.

By doing this, you will come to realize through personal experience that we have all been endowed by the Creator with the power to heal the world and transform it into a better condition.

It has long been said that God helps those who help themselves. What this means is that God does not so much reach out into the world to change it: You do. You are here as a free agent, equipped with free will to affect the world for better or worse. You can make the world a better place.

With a powerful tool for world healing at your disposal, you can become a shining light in the ongoing chronicle of humankind's transformation into the New Reality.

The Secret to World Transformation

The Secret to World Transformation

In England in the 1950's, a spiritual master called George King was deeply concerned with the continually escalating Cold War tensions between America and the Soviet Union. His ability to reach the deepest states of consciousness meant that he could clearly see the mounting and very real risk of global nuclear annihilation. He was also able to envision how people could make enough of a difference in the balance of world thought to bring the situation back into the safety zone.

He developed a powerful technique of world healing whereby people would set an intention of world peace and enlightenment and then radiate it energetically into the world as spiritual light. By using life energy as a carrier wave for spiritual intentions, people became capable of transforming the global mind atmosphere in a distinct and positive manner.

He pointed out that there is a strategic subtlety to this method of world healing. When you practice it, you give away the energy of your inspiration and that creates a vacuum within you. Then, nature must fill that vacuum. However – and here is the subtlety – you are not just filling yourself with inspiring power and then giving it away, only to see it immediately replaced.

The very act of spiritual service to others raises your frequency of consciousness one step at a time, every time you perform such an act.

World healing, in itself, is a spiritual path and it is a path which delivers sure and balanced results. When you tread such a path, you *will* – not may – make great strides in your spiritual growth.

The world lacks spiritual light because, even though the supply of life energy is plentiful, people generally don't know how to condition and use it.

The universal supply of life energy has to be first conditioned with spiritual intent in order to affect others and transform the global mind atmosphere which surrounds this planet. By sending streams of spiritually-conditioned life energy out into the world, you create more peace and upliftment in the world. The energy is always there, in a state of potential, ready to use, but it has to be conditioned and sent out to humanity in order to bring about healing.

Personally, I always think of world healing as a kind of spiritual double rewards program: It brings spiritual advancement to you and the world, and it also changes your karmic pattern.

Like a magnetic influence in an aura that surrounds you, your karmic pattern consists of the sum consciousness of everything that you are – everything you have ever thought, felt, done, or experienced. As you travel through life, the world reacts to you in accordance with that signature energy which exists around you.

If you are a helpful type of person, you will experience a reality which is generally helpful. If you offer your love and support to the world as a service without expectation, then your life will become filled with love and support. If you help the world advance spiritually, you will find that personal spiritual advancement comes more easily than ever.

All of this is automatic because life in the universe was designed to act like a mirror.

Being lucky in life is no accident. Help the world and the world helps you.

Heal the World

Heal the World and Make it a Better Place

The World Healing Technique is an easy-to-learn and effective method which uses the principles of the original King Technique to heal the world by attracting, conditioning, and radiating spiritual energy. This technique can be practiced virtually at any time, anywhere. Whenever you can close your eyes for a few moments and focus on your inner resources, you can take the opportunity to heal the world.

Here are the principles that form the foundation of this world-changing spiritual technique:

Healing energy is also called universal life energy, and it is available to you at all times. It comes from the center of the universe, through the Sun, and fills all of the space around you. On a sunny day, when its presence is especially intense, your eyes can often faintly detect globules of this energy floating in the air as you look up towards the clear sky.

As a non-physical etheric form of energy, universal life energy responds immediately to applied mental pressure. This means that you can use your faculty of imagination to apply mental pressure to attract, condition, and radiate this energy. You can use life energy as a carrier energy for the transmission of your mental and spiritual intentions.

Recognizing your spiritual nature raises your consciousness to a higher frequency and therefore gives you access to greater healing power. At the start of each healing session, take the time to remember that you are a spiritual being living in a physical world. Take the opportunity to look upwards to higher realms of consciousness and ask God or the universal Spirit for the life energy that you are about to use. The energy is there for you to use whether you ask or not, but the act of asking lifts your mind above the material world and forges a spiritual connection between you and the higher realms.

Be sure to add heart-centered feeling to your spiritual thoughts. Gratitude is a powerful inducer of unconditional love, so give thanks to the Creator for universal life energy, for everything that you love about your life, and for existence itself. This spiritual connection of heart and mind will raise your frequency of consciousness and this amplifies your healing efforts many times.

Heart-centered consciousness is focused in the heart chakra, or energy center, which is located outside of your physical body approximately four inches (ten centimeters) in front of the breastbone. Like all chakras, the front-facing heart chakra is a small, whirling vortex of energy operating at a specific frequency of consciousness.

Universal life energy is best visualized as white light because that consists of a combination of all frequencies of etheric light energy and is, therefore, the most balanced in its general healing power.

The universe reflects who you are. When you practice healing the world, by automatic reflection, you heal who you are. Any and all issues which have been challenging for you will tend to move towards resolution as you help the world in this way.

The World Healing Technique

The World Healing Technique

Try the World Healing Technique now and see what a difference it makes to your spiritual life, both immediately and, as a reaction, in the following days.

There's nothing quite as uplifting as starting your day by sending healing energy to the world. It brightens your day and makes it feel good to be alive.

Sit upright, preferably with your hands resting in your lap, palms facing upwards. Breathe rhythmically and evenly. Close your eyes and turn away from your everyday thoughts by letting your attention focus on your breath. Whenever you notice your thoughts wandering, peacefully turn away from those thoughts, which can always be dealt with later, and return to focusing on your breath.

Recognize your spiritual nature. Know that you are a spiritual being living in a physical world and ask God or the universal Spirit for the life energy that you are about to use. Give gratitude to the Creator for universal life energy, for everything that you love about your life, and for existence itself. This connection to higher consciousness will amplify your efforts many times.

Take several breaths. With each in-breath, visualize life energy building into a vibrant white light within you and charging every cell of your being with its life-giving energy.

First, visualize the positive change that you want to bring into being in the world. Even though you are healing something that you perceive as negative, it is important to focus, instead, on the desired positive outcome. If you send energy to something negative, you will amplify its power. By sending energy conditioned for a positive outcome, you make that form of healing possible.

For example, in your mind's eye, instead of a world suffering from strife, visualize the people of the world at peace. When you think of world peace, what is the first symbol that springs to mind – a crowd of happy children, a world without borders? Use that symbol, or, if pictures don't easily come to mind, simply use the words, *world peace*, as the focus for your intention.

Or, instead of seeing spiritual ignorance and the suffering that it prolongs, visualize people who are becoming enlightened by spiritual understanding. Use the first picture that comes to mind or the words, *world enlightenment*.

Or, as another example, instead of seeing people displaced and distraught from a recent catastrophe, you could see aid workers being successful in their efforts to bring relief and medical assistance to those people, or use the words, *energy to the aid workers*.

Now, we're ready to use the inbreath-outbreath cycle to transmit healing energy for the specified purpose. With every inbreath, see your lungs being filled with the vibrant white light of universal life energy.

With every outbreath, send the power of this love and light out to humanity. Direct it as a beam of brilliant white light from your heart chakra out into the world, holding the intention of healing.

Perform this as a series of inbreaths and outbreaths for as long as you wish, then relax and spend some time in the afterglow of a spiritual mission well accomplished.

These are the days of action, and that means service to others. Even better, your service to others also helps you in your own spiritual enlightenment. Action and reaction are opposite and equal.

Every time you send your light out into the world, you take another step forward towards your own enlightenment.

To learn how to amplify your world healing efforts and further study the science of effective world healing, see the free *In-Depth Guide to World Healing* at the website InfiniteBeing.com.

The World Healing Technique in summary

Sit upright with your eyes closed.

Make a spiritual connection, one which includes gratitude for life.

Intend world healing by visualizing the desired positive outcome.

Breathe in life energy with each inbreath.

On each outbreath, repeat your intention and send a beam of white light from your heart to your intended destination.

The Inner Light That Beckons

The Inner Light That Beckons

Because the primary purpose of life is growth in consciousness, sooner or later everyone begins to sense the spiritual light that lies within their inner being.

The intuitive sensing of this light heals your spirit and beckons you forward into the realms of more light. When this happens, you are firmly on the path of spiritual growth. No longer searching for the meaning of life, you are heading with determination along your path to the state of consciousness from which you originally came.

Your inner nature is unconditional happiness because within your true being lies a wellspring of joy. It is your birthright to discover this inner source of joy and inspiration.

The three-step technique to spiritual development in *Spirituality Made Simple* opens the doorway to positive and lasting transformation. *Look Up, Look In, Look Out* is literally as easy as *1-2-3*.

Look Up with your mind
Look In through your heart
Look Out and create a better world

The surest way to advance yourself spiritually is to give spiritual service to a world that is in desperate need of your light and your inspiration.

With your head in the heavens and your heart aflame with the natural desire to help others, send waves of healing power out into the world to hasten its transformation into the emerging New Reality.

Today, we are making history in a pivotal time that will be celebrated for centuries to come. Be a part of the Great Transformation of our times and be sure to tell others who could benefit from engaging in the uplifting practice of healing the world.

The surest way to spiritual growth and a life filled with purpose is to heal the world and make it a better place.

Tell a friend, tell all your friends, tell the world.

Together, we will create a world of beauty, peace and wonder.

Further Resources

Further Resources

Owen Waters is the author of many articles, books and e-books on spirituality. His teachings display a rare clarity of understanding and provide an inspiring vision of the emerging New Reality. For an up-to-date list of his books, visit InfiniteBeing.com.

He also writes a complimentary spiritual metaphysics newsletter which empowers people to discover new vistas of inspiration, love and creativity. To receive an inspiring new article on spiritual metaphysics each weekend, sign up for his free newsletter at:

www.infinitebeing.com/news

17524635R00077

Made in the USA
Lexington, KY
13 September 2012